WYOMING

Also by Terry McDonell

CALIFORNIA BLOODSTOCK

THE RIDE

Published simultaneously in Canada
Printed by in the United States of America by RR Donnelley

ISBN 978-0-8021-4500-0.

FIRST EDITION

Grove Press
www.groveatlantic.com
Distributed by Publishers Group West

Designed by Neil Jamieson
Photographs by Jean Pagliuso
Thanks Bob Kanell

STACEY

WYOMING

THE LOST POEMS

BY TERRY McDONELL

*These poems were written in
the 1970s in Wyoming and
Montana; some slightly later in
New York City and California.*

CONTENTS

I. WYOMING

II. COASTS

I

WYOMING

Oil Field Trash and Proud of It
— T-Shirt Slogan, 1979

BOOMTOWN GIRL I

She wrote:

(to the man)
I keep
Thinking about seeing you drive away
That next morning, and it
Didn't hit me that it was you
Leaving or I'd have jumped out
Chased you down.
Stupid girl.
You know, if I'm bothering you
You can just tell me.
I'm not sweet and I'm sick of all this heartland.
People always checking in
Following rule and line.

I want to drift.
I want to go to Phoenix. With you
Find the side of the tracks
Where they sell religious
Artifacts, nite light Virgin Marys.
Am I in trouble?
Do you really want to meet me in Minneapolis?
Or somewhere else? I get
The feeling that you can't get away. Ever
And I miss your hands on me. Am I
Ever going to get that again?

BOOMTOWN GIRL II

She wrote:

(to the man)
Brace yourself
I've been drinking again.
My days take a pattern.
I wake up, I think it's not okay
to write some burning message
Then finally I'm seething
And I want you next to me
With your head on my boy chest, and I
Want to pet you with my fingernails
Like a cat and be under you like that.
And then I want to touch your face and your back
And kiss your forehead and drink
You deep and slow, like my bourbon.
You, you crack me up.
I'm wasting away
And you crack me up.

BOOMTOWN GIRL III

She wrote:

(to the man)
Hey, just so you know
I've got a little incentive for you.
I've been thinking about you differently
So you can forget any airport scene
All romantic slow-motion.
I'm sure you don't really know
What to do with me, though, so
I'll be hitting Desperados tonight
That country thump dance club
Where they have the live bull riding
I told you about
Lots of cowboys. Maybe
I'll think of you more
And more with each little sip.
Maybe not
And, I mean, just to be honest,
Did I mention our abortion?

A CHANGE OF PLANS

Take care to sell your horse before he dies
The art of life is passing losses on
                    — Robert Frost, "The Ingenuities of Debt"

Are you still thinking of destinations for me?
Like home? Back to you? Know what? I was
Looking at my Rand McNally
Figuring miles and stops
At the same time you were talking
About getting new furniture. Made me
Almost want you again, like high school.
Didn't last. I am running around in love
With Russell now. Remember him
From the Lone Star?
And I don't want to stop
Come home again for the usual.
I always liked Denver
More than you, and I'm staying.

THERE WAS A PHOTOGRAPH

There was a photograph
That made the rounds. Me naked
I don't know why I let him take it.
What was I thinking?

The day I bought the gun
I showed it to him, only him
Told him I might sleep
with the barrel in my mouth.
He said he'd like to get a Polaroid.

The cops came right away. Just like TV
Except they weren't very nice to me.

WHAT IT TAKES TO
GET OUT OF GILETTE

Marietta
(her real name)
Forlorn Wyoming oil field girl
Drinking after hours
In the B&T (Building & Trades) Club
Across that big dirt lot
Behind the Casper Hilton
Locks eyes with herself
In the mirror, thinks:
I used to be fucked up on drugs
Then I got fucked up on Jesus
Now I am thirsty...

THE COWBOY BAR & MUSEUM

I'm doing laundry now. *Yee haw.*
Getting ready to drive on
Up to Cody. I'm going
Through Fromberg and will stop
At the Cowboy Bar & Museum
(one & the same)
On my way.
It's pretty hilarious. You would love it.
All that irony you think
Is so cool. If you
Ever get your ass out here
I'll pay your admission
buy your shot
So you won't make me
Feel like such a whore
Again.

TROUBLE IN SHOSHONE

The deputy went
To the Covered Wagon Trailer Court
On two calls:
A dog had been shot with a .22
The other a domestic situation
A woman beating on her husband
For shooting her dog.

VEGAS

She would like you to send the check
By Thursday, please
Or better
You could wire the money
So she won't have to wait
For anything to clear.

CROW GIRL IN A BAR IN SHERIDAN

I would have stolen you
From your father
And you would be with me
Now, still, on the plains.

DRINKER

Susan McBride Cahill 1948 — 1998

Big drinker but never confused
You were a riot of judgment.
Racing from summit to summit and across the moors
Of your special reading, in the worst possible weather
And sometimes into the night, making everything
Especially the cliffs behind your house, more interesting.

The wilder the better, but sober you could barely walk a mile
Couldn't make it into the backcountry, the high windy places
The places where rock and water and sky can take your breath
Where the landscape hammers your eyes.
You never made it there
You always went looking for trouble in town
        —committing experience, McGuane called it.
You said the true nature of wildness eludes us all.
That changed the way we saw the world, that time in Mexico
All of us going fishing, leaving you on the porch
With your bourbon and enough ice
Your own direct connection with the unforgiving
Balance of nature, not jumping
Like us, out of airplanes to get your rush.

RIDER

Kathy Flynn Jourdane 1945 — 1974

The morning the doctor told her
How it was going to be she told him
It was her life not his and she would decide.
The craziness is what I like best
About myself, she said. So what if
My sleep is full of dirt.
I cultivate it. If you could only see
Me naked in my garden.
Hey, some girls, yes they do go wild
The ache, the longing, the sureness of that first time
Makes them unfit for domestication
Makes them want to ride away.

At dusk, she picked her way through dwarf shrubforms
Clustered in tight packs on the gray underslope
Of the Tehachapi Mountains. Later, in the moonlight
Their shadows seemed almost human, apelike
An army of monkeys or midgets
Standing guard in the night as she made her camp.

On her back counting stars for comfort
She dreamed of growing things, shapes and textures
Pushing and sliding against each other, trying
To break free. And all around her she felt
The large movements of men and horses.

When they began looking for her she woke up.
She looked across the dying fire, waiting
Wide awake, waiting, until she heard
A scraping beneath the folded mountains, teeth perhaps
Tearing into the earth somewhere under the crust.

Soon she was climbing again, higher into the mountains
Riding up and away, into how it was going to be.

WAR PARTY

The army dead were removed to the military cemetery
at Little Big Horn; the Nez Perce remain where they fell.

I keep saying Crazy Horse
but I mean Chief Joseph. You think
I don't remember our picnic? You took me
That time. Right there
where he handed over his Winchester after
Two thousand ponies gone and I knew
How he felt. I'm telling you
A friend of mine
She bought a Smith & Wesson
At the mercantile and shot
Herself yesterday.
Dead. She's 29. Or was.
Looked like a china doll
In a cowboy hat barrel racing
Her ass off. That poor family
I honestly just can't
Even imagine. Fuck.

BACK IN CALIFORNIA

Poncho Valenzuela, fourteen
Climbing into a ring, fighting
The same year he found out
About his father and his sister
And a lot of other things he told me
I didn't want to know.
He's in jail now, still.

Then Fillmore Cross, Gypsy Joker
Dead, chopped into pieces by the Angles
Up on Skyline Boulevard. We burned a house down
Up there once. Got away in a stolen car. Wild
Because wild was the best way to be. Except
Not really. It didn't matter, not at all
None of it, until years later.

II
Eucalyptus on the wind
Over an empty beach.
Now a woman coming, then another going
Walking the wet sand alone
Not a pretty story either one
You can always tell.

Things go wrong in California. Some people
Are off. Women look at you, smile
Endless smiles of sunshine acid
Back there somewhere hiding
What they want and something else
A drug deal they remember
From that horrible summer
They never want to hear about again.

III
August 8, 1969, warm night
Charlie Manson and his crazy chics
Pull up in front of Sharon Tate's house
Back in California.

DANCING BACKWARDS

Can you really do that?
Just slip and slide
Snake yourself
Out of those boot jeans
Dancing backwards
Toward the bed?

ELKO GIRL

So where's your heart today, Mr. Cowboy?
This is what she says to him
To open up the day
Works every time.

Used it first back when
A new girl in town
Fancy boots
A gardening dress
Makes her way
Through the Greyhound depot
Starts a new life
In the first bar on the left.

FINDING A WIFE IN WYOMING

Lonely rancher on isolated 3,000 acres needs wife to enjoy
ranch, help with the cattle, keep track of me on cold winter
nights. Good sense of humor as important as good figure.

— Lander Gazette, 1979

She watches him move
Showing her around.

Hills roll away from the house
Set in a notch where the mountain starts
The nearest neighbor five miles South.
Bottomland spreads
Where a small river cuts through
An old Lakota camp.

One of those deals where you buy a place
Work it, prove up as soon as you can
Trade up, do it again. He did that
Every three years since he was twenty
Pulling four-day summer shifts in the Gas Hills
To keep it all moving.

Winters I just like to stay at home, he says
Enjoy the ranch.

She looks at his hands, says
I will marry you.

II

COASTS

I don't need any hurricane warnings
over the seven a.m. news-and-weather
to tell me today will be a bad day
— Sylvia Plath

COWBOY MOVIE

Don Simpson, long gone
And Patty Detroit

It is raining on a lake
The door to the motel room is open
A television screen flickers
A fat man snores on the bed
A woman with a withered hand walks into Cartier
Asks to see the most expensive rings
A limousine speeds across the badlands
A seaplane lands on the lake and taxis to a small dock.
What?
Midnight
Breaking into a car she doesn't own
In a ranch yard 200 miles from the nearest airport
Is a girl from New York
In Wyoming for twenty-one hours.
Not another coke movie.

OFF-SEASON

Flat sea, flat air. High clouds again
Side by side in beach chairs, watching
Frigate birds hovering in the white sky.

Day five with no wind.
Nobody comes now.

She wants to know what they're doing
Here off season. She is starting
Starting to not want to eat anything
Ever again, just get high
Maybe fly like those birds
But not here.

He walks naked to the bungalow
Calls his service. Messages
From people who don't matter.

Out the window, she hasn't moved.
She never moves.

He makes some calls, leaves messages.
Gives them an area code to think about
When they get back from Ketchum
Or wherever.

They go to dinner behind a stucco wall
Through a pastel door, patio,
A table under an old hibiscus tree.
It's the only nice place open.
Now they are sitting
Facing, looking through
Each other like broken windows.

SOME GIRL HE MET

She told him about a date she had
        with a woman
In another life, where the fabric
Was too soft for her.
        She had to cry
For all she did and did not do
For all the lost sex for no reason
        as sex should be
Except the color of it somehow, the muted blush
And all that softness turned it into
        something else
Like prancing queers in some green room
Somewhere explaining fashion to each other.
        And she was not ever
A lesbian, how could she be? Wanting
Him now so much.

FRENCH GIRL

A cliché, smoking in the restaurant
Reading the new fashion
Laughing at America.
It's modern men, *ha*
They have no cock, she said
They don't (make you) want
To fuck anybody.
What is the point, anyway?
Art is sex in the afternoon.
All the women of Paris know that
Especially the ones who go to the galleries, like me
You can smell it on us.

ALL YOU WOULD HAVE TO DO

What if we all behaved like you
Screaming, screaming, screaming
Liar, liar, liar! at the best table
In the front room at Spago.

Say, just say, for the sake of this
Argument (mutually repellent voices)
You were sorry, you were sick
For a while, not feeling well
Not yourself. No dress to wear
No place to go anyway. No friends
You had forgotten something important.

Later, I got your message
Call back right away
You might not be alive, there
Where you couldn't live
Without a dress or friends
And no place to go
Because I was so mean
I turned off the phone.

Morning now and I have listened
To your new messages wondering
 If you are dead yet
(sky falling on Malibu)
Or resting with you medecine.

Say, just say, that everyone
Would understand. They would forgive
You. They would call you back.
They would love you still. But
 Not me.

MYKONOS, 1968

Just back from Greece
Her hair various
Shades of blond and cut
Very short, close to her face
Except for a scalp lock
That sweeps across her cheek.
Her tattoo, tiny secret, on one of her breasts
Gave her a small reputation on Mikonos
Fuck Mykonos.

OLDER MEN

You can only do so much, she said
I married a much older man.

They all drank scotch
Made money, pocket squares
Folded into their pinstripes, real estate
Deals lined up like long putts at Augusta
(You had to know your sports).

They lied about everything
Except how beautiful I was.
Creamy girl, drunk girl, dirty
Dirty girl in bed
On a 42-foot custom Hatteras
Out of Lyford Cay.

Then one day I had to help him out of a cab.
In the end, how I look at it is
I took him shopping.

GIVE HER A CALL

I know you know
She's sort of in shock
Going to talk to no one
About any of it but I
Happen to know
She would love to talk to you.
You have her home number, no?

I know, I know she's acting
The *grande dame*
Of pain, which is un-cool
On a girl with so much jewelry.
Did I say girl? Anyway
If you don't mind me saying, I think
She'd be a catch
Classy and connected, fun in the sack
even sweet
I've heard
When she's not like this.

THE CAUSE

After Dawn Powell on Pauline Hemingway, 1942

She seemed sharp-edged, too eager, brown and desperate
Her confessionals, her rosaries, that kept her head up
During the bad years
Did not fill the hole in her life
Gave it a frittering quality
That did not flatter.

Like her you should have a cause, beyond your Prada
And your crazy husband with his new strong women
And a philosophy instead
Of a religion that lets you worship
At your mirror.

LADY OF THE CANYON

Did you really
Leave your baby girl behind
To sing in clubs
Give her away
To do lines with studio musicians?

Remember her?
She remembers you
With your painting colors on your face
And your men's room highs
And the money you made and how
You bought her back with it.

She thinks you are doing just fine
Without the truth.

DANGER GIRL

Right now, somewhere, you are forgetting me
— Jason Shinder, "The Future"

You are in Africa
With your liquid skin and your perfect
Biting mouth. A country, a dark continent of yourself
Within a country of dirt within a continent darker than imagined
Or thought about in bed with me, anxious to leave
Then drinking away the afternoon. Are you safe there now
Without me or any man you might want sometime
If you ever come home.

PARTY GIRL

At the party, crowded
Across the room
Picking him out with her eyes.

And later, at a bar, talking
About herself like a painting she saw once
In a small museum, in Paris
Abstract
Impossible to describe.

Then out on the street:
I want, she said, to know
If you glow in the dark.

A MAN WHO THINKS ABOUT WOMEN

A man who thinks about women
Thinks about more than women
He thinks:
First clouds then rain then
All the strange weather in the universe
Between who she is and who
She claims to be.

FASHION WEEK

(Out the window)
Modern boats running
On flat water at night
Approximate the supernatural.
Things happen beneath the surface
Of the East River or at a party.

Careful light on good art
Gives the loft order, serenity
A small Cezanne in the entry hall.
In the powder room a model explains
To a lawyer she slept with in college
Coke is no problem if you're careful.

She needs a break from what
you see in this town.
On a shoot, Union Square
Farmers' Market those people
Giving away their dogs. Sadness
Like that.

MEMORY STARTS

Irma Saphronia Nelson McDonell Elden Edwards 1919 — 2004

Memory starts with a pretty girl with nice legs
Getting out of a Ford convertible
On the edge of a cherry orchard in 1949.

Young husband dead, shot down, gone.
A trunk full of uniforms and she would show
The medals to her son and he would turn
The wings over in his tiny hands.

She must have been exhausted
By the time she got there, to California
And just settled into it, her new life
With relief.

Everyone (the men) in construction
Or working fruit and row crops
While she was teaching school.
A good job that didn't depend on the weather.

And out the window
Apricot and cherry blossoms
Just beyond the playground
And in the sky
P-41s going down in flame.